To Sarah + Johnny,

Just to let you have a glimpse of our city and its surrounds.
Hopefully it will entice you to visit us one day.
We hope 2004 will be a great year for us all.

Love

Liz, Melanie + Louis

Jan 2004

D1299448

SPECTACULAR

CAPE TOWN

SPECTACULAR

CAPE TOWN

TIM O'HAGAN

Struik Publishers
(a division of New Holland Publishing
(South Africa) (Pty) Ltd)

Cornelis Struik House   Garfield House
 80 McKenzie Street   86–88 Edgware Road
Cape Town 8001   LONDON W2 2EA
South Africa   United Kingdom
www.struik.co.za   **www.newhollandpublishers.com**

14 Aquatic Drive   218 Lake Road
Frenchs Forest   Northcote, Auckland
NSW 2086, Australia   New Zealand

10 9 8 7 6 5 4 3 2 1

Publishing manager: Annlerie van Rooyen
Design director: Janice Evans
Designer: Illana Fridkin
Managing editor: Lesley Hay-Whitton
Project co-ordinator: Glynne Newlands
French translator: Jean-Paul Houssière
German translator: Friedel Herrmann
Cartographer: Steven Felmore

ISBN 1 86872 679 7

Reproduction by Hirt & Carter Cape (Pty) Ltd
Printed and bound in Hong Kong by Sing Cheong
Printing Company Limited

The cosmopolitan hub of the Western Cape, Cape Town is the gateway to South and southern Africa – and, for many visitors, to the vast continent of Africa itself. It's not surprising that many of South Africa's most popular tourist attractions are in and around Cape Town. A city of spectacular natural beauty, it is also a centre of culture and history. The exquisite photographs in this book highlight the unique qualities and fusion of cultures of the city – from Victorian architecture and fine Cape Dutch homesteads, to Muslim *kramats* that dot the mountainside, a memorial to the lives of the slaves brought from East Asia. Opulent suburbs are a short distance from townships, where it's not unusual to find cattle grazing alongside the road. Street traders sell unique hand-made crafts from across Africa on the doorstep of international corporations. The photographs in *Spectacular Cape Town* vividly capture the atmosphere of vibrant festivity created by the combination of upmarket shops, craftmarkets, art galleries, restaurants, theatres and live music in the city. The author of this magnificent volume is to be congratulated for bringing this unique region to life, not only for those who already know the Cape, but for those who have yet to experience its many splendours.

Dr Mike Fabricius

CEO Western Cape Tourism Board

June 2001

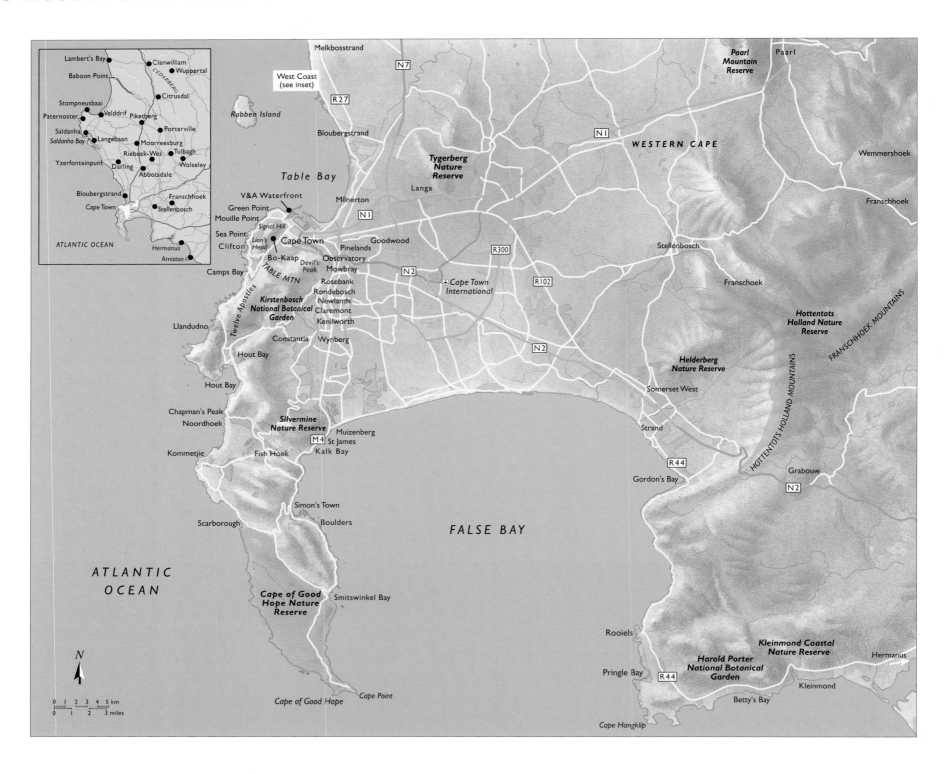

ATLANTIC OCEAN

Lambert's Bay
Baboon Point
Clanwilliam
Wuppertal
CEDARBERG
Citrusdal
Stompneusbaai
Velddrif
Piketberg
Paternoster
Saldanha
Porterville
Saldanha Bay
Langebaan
Moorreesburg
Riebeek-Wes
Tulbagh
Yzerfonteinpunt
Darling
Abbotsdale
Wolseley
Blouwbergstrand
Franschhoek
Cape Town
Stellenbosch
Hermanus
Arniston

West Coast
(see inset)

Melkbosstrand

Paarl Mountain Reserve
Paarl

N7
R27
N1
WESTERN CAPE
Wemmershoek
Robben Island
Blouwbergstrand
Tygerberg Nature Reserve
Franschhoek
Table Bay
Langa
V&A Waterfront
Milnerton
Green Point
Mouille Point
N1
Signal Hill
Sea Point
Cape Town
Goodwood
Stellenbosch
Clifton
Lion's Head
Bo-Kaap
Observatory
Pinelands
R300
Devil's Peak
Mowbray
N2
Cape Town International
R102
Camps Bay
TABLE MTN
Rosebank
Franschoek
Twelve Apostles
Kirstenbosch National Botanical Garden
Rondebosch
Newlands
Claremont
Hottentots Holland Nature Reserve
Llandudno
Kenilworth
Constantia
Wynberg
Hout Bay
Helderberg Nature Reserve
Hout Bay
N2
Somerset West
Chapman's Peak
Silvermine Nature Reserve
Muizenberg
Strand
Noordhoek
M4
St James
Kalk Bay
Kommetjie
Fish Hoek
Gordon's Bay
R44
Simon's Town
Scarborough
Boulders
FALSE BAY
Grabouw
N2
ATLANTIC OCEAN
Rooiels
Kleinmond Coastal Nature Reserve
Cape of Good Hope Nature Reserve
Smitswinkel Bay
Pringle Bay
R44
Harold Porter National Botanical Garden
Hermanus
Kleinmond
Cape of Good Hope
Cape Point
Betty's Bay
Cape Hangklip

HOTTENTOTS HOLLAND MOUNTAINS
FRANSCHHOEK MOUNTAINS

N

0 1 2 3 4 5 km
0   1   2   3 miles

In the southwest corner of the African continent ramparts of sandstone rise majestically above a canvas of shimmering blue, announcing one of the world's most beautiful cities – Cape Town. Here, beneath the lofty presence of Table Mountain, a crooked finger of land curves southward into the Atlantic, revealing bays of ivory sand and wild floral gardens that tumble down to the water's edge. In 1580 Sir Francis Drake called this region 'the fairest Cape in all the world'. And early Dutch and Portuguese explorers who followed were so awed by the beauty of this untamed coastline that many decided to stay. From a huddle of makeshift huts established at the Cape by Dutch Commander Jan van Riebeeck in 1652, Cape Town has grown into a cosmopolitan colossus, with satellite suburbs hugging the slopes of mountains which have helped create the richest floral kingdom on earth. A wide diversity of cultures has found a home in this natural Eden, revelling in the sun-soaked beaches, botanical gardens, hiking trails and other outdoor attractions a few minutes' drive from the city centre. State-of-the-art pleasure domes, such as Ratanga Junction and Grand West Casino, vie with shopping complexes like Century City and craftmarkets such as that at Greenmarket Square, while the dockside ambience of the V&A Waterfront and the delights of the wine routes are perennially popular. For those with more eclectic interests there are museums, outdoor theatres and historical sites testifying to Cape Town's rich cultural history. Amid these attractions are the special jewels of the Mother City – the parks, gardens and natural sanctuaries – among them the Cape of Good Hope Nature Reserve, Kirstenbosch National Botanical Garden and Rondevlei Bird Sanctuary. More than 300 years after it was founded, Cape Town still remains the pearl of the southern seas.

Au-dessus des eaux scintillantes de l'océan qui encerclent la pointe méridionale du continent africain, s'élèvent de majestueux remparts de grès, marquant l'une des plus belles villes du monde – Cape Town. Ici, du pied de Table Mountain, une langue de terre s'élance dans l'Atlantique, dont les vagues déferlent sur un littoral aux sables d'ivoire longé d'étendues de fleurs sauvages. En 1580, Sir Francis Drake nomma l'endroit 'le cap le plus beau du monde'. Plus tard, quand les premiers explorateurs hollandais et portugais retracèrent ses pas, ils furent tellement impressionnés que nombre d'entre eux décidèrent de s'y établir. Des cahutes précaires érigées au Cap par le gouverneur hollandais Jan Van Riebeeck en 1652, Cape Town est devenue une métropole cosmopolite dont les faubourgs se blottissent au pied de montagnes qui ont été proclamées le plus riche royaume floral sur terre. Une grande diversité de cultures se retrouvent dans cet Eden, jouissant des plages ensoleillées, des jardins botaniques, des randonnées dans les montagnes et de nombreuses autres activités de plein air, toutes à deux pas du centre-ville. Des attractions ultramodernes telles que Ratanga Junction et Grand West Casino rivalisent avec des centres commerciaux comme Century City ou encore le marché en plein air de Greenmarket Square, sans compter le V&A Waterfront et la Wine Route dont les délices seront toujours énormément populaires. Témoignant du riche patrimoine de Cape Town, les nombreux musées, théâtres en plein air et sites historiques attireront les esprits plus éclectiques. Et, parmi toutes ces attractions se trouvent les joyaux tout spéciaux de la 'Mother City' – les parcs, jardins fleuris et réserves naturelles. Plus de 300 ans après sa fondation, Cape Town continue d'être la perle de l'Afrique.

Am südwestlichen Zipfel des afrikanischen Kontinents erheben sich Sandsteinbastionen majestätisch aus dem leuchtenden Blau und zeigen eine der schönsten Städte der Welt an – Kapstadt. Hier, zu Füßen des imposanten Tafelberges, streckt sich ein krummer Finger aus Fels und Sand südwärts in den Atlantik. Helle Sandstrände und Naturgärten aus Wildblumen entfalten sich bis ans Meeresufer. 1580 nannte Sir Frances Drake diese Region 'das schönste Kap im Erdenrund'. Portugiesische und holländische Entdeckungsreisende waren so beeindruckt von der ungezähmten Naturschönheit dieser Küste, daß letztere sich entschlossen, hier eine Niederlassung zu gründen. Die kleine Ansiedlung mit kauernden Hütten, die 1652 angelegt wurde, ist herangewachsen zu einem kosmopolitischen Koloß, Kapstadt, dessen Vororte und Satellitenstädte sich an die Bergkette schmiegen, die eines der vielfältigsten Florenreiche auf Erden hervorgebracht hatte. In diesem Naturparadies haben sich Menschen verschiedener Kulturen eine Heimat geschaffen, und sie erfreuen sich an sonnigen Stränden, Wanderwegen und anderen Freizeitattraktionen in freier Natur. Viele davon liegen nur wenige Autominuten vom Stadtkern entfernt. Moderne Unterhaltungsparks, wie Ratanga Junction oder das Grand West Kasino, wetteifern mit Einkaufszentren und Straßenmärkten. Die Hafenambiente der V&A Waterfront und die Genüsse der Weinstraßen erfreuen sich zu allen Zeiten großer Beliebtheit. Auch für andere Interessen ist gesorgt; es gibt Museen, Freilichttheater und historische Stätten. Und natürlich die Juwelen der Mutterstadt - wie das Naturschutzgebiet an der Kapspitze und der botanische Garten von Kirstenbosch. Noch immer ist Kapstadt die Perle der südlichen Meere.

THE MOTHER CITY

Flanked by Devil's peak on the left and Lion's Head on the right, the rocky pediments of Table Mountain tower above Cape Town.

Flanquée par Devil's Peak à gauche et Lion's Head à droite, la masse rocheuse de Table Mountain domine Cape Town.

Mit der Teufelsspitze zur Linken und dem Löwenkopf zur Rechten bildet der Tafelberg einen Ziergiebel oberhalb Kapstadts.

AERIAL ACROBAT

With nerves of steel and a head for heights, a bungee jumper gets his kicks by throwing himself out of a Table Mountain cable car, approximately 600 metres above the ground.

Armé de nerfs d'acier et n'éprouvant aucun vertige, un sauteur à l'élastique se jette du téléphérique de Table Mountain à 600 mètres de hauteur.

Nerven von Stahl und keine Höhenängste muß der Bungee-Springer haben, der sich aus 600m Höhe aus der Seilbahngondel stürzt.

MOUNTAIN VIEWPOINT

An observation platform on the summit of Table Mountain (ABOVE) affords tourists a panoramic view of Table Bay and the gentle contours of the coast-line sweeping north to Milnerton and Bloubergstrand. Visitors amble along walkways on top of the mountain (OPPOSITE), a wonderland of indigenous vegetation and meandering streams.

MOUNTAIN MEANDER

Du sommet de Table Mountain (CI-CONTRE) les touristes peuvent admirer un panorama s'étendant de Table Bay jusqu'à Milnerton et Bloubergstrand vers le nord. En haut de la montagne, des sentiers mènent les visiteurs dans un paysage enchanté de végétation indigène, traversé de ruisseaux (CI-DESSUS).

Ein Aussichtsplatz auf dem Tafelberg (GEGENÜBER) bietet Touristen einen Panoramablick über die Tafelbucht und die Küste, die sich in sanftem Bogen nordwärts nach Milnerton und Bloubergstrand hinzieht. Die Besucher spazieren auf den Fußwegen oben auf dem Berg. Es ist ein Paradies mit einheimischer Pflanzenwelt und kleinen Bachläufen (OBEN).

SHOP AT THE TOP

Nestling among the granite rocks at the summit of Table Mountain, a shop and restaurant (ABOVE) offer visitors an opportunity to browse and relax above the Atlantic Ocean's shimmering canvas of blue. A bar at the upper cable station (OPPOSITE) keeps visitors entertained while they wait for their ride down in the cable car to the lower cable station.

TABLE MOUNTAIN PUB

Nichés dans la rocaille au sommet de Table Mountain, un magasin et un restaurant (CI-CONTRE) offrent aux visiteurs l'occasion de se relaxer en admirant les eaux bleues et scintillantes de l'Atlantique. A la station terminale du téléphérique, un bar est ouvert aux visiteurs (CI-DESSUS) qui attendent de s'embarquer pour la descente.

Zwischen den Granitfelsen auf dem Tafelberg bieten ein Laden und ein Restaurant (GEGENÜBER) Besuchern die Gelegenheit zum gemütlichen Einkauf und zur erholsamen Rast oberhalb der ausgedehnten, schimmernden blauen Fläche des Atlantik. Die Bar an der oberen Talstation (OBEN) bietet ein unterhaltsames Umfeld für diejenigen, die darauf warten, mit der Seilbahn wieder abwärts zu schweben.

TWILIGHT PAGEANT

SUNDOWN LOOKOUT

Seen from Table Mountain, streetlights illuminating Cape Town's city bowl fuse with the colours of a dying day.

Vues du haut de Table Mountain, les lumières de Cape Town se fusionnent avec les couleurs du crépuscule.

Zu Füssen liegt die Stadt, wo Straßenbeleuchtung und Dämmerlicht miteinander verschmelzen.

THE LIVING MOUNTAIN – FLORA

Table Mountain is sanctuary to a colourful array of indigenous flora, including cone bushes (TOP LEFT), crassulas (TOP RIGHT), ericas (ABOVE LEFT) and pincushion proteas (ABOVE RIGHT). Among the fauna found on the mountain are these engaging rock rabbits or dassies (OPPOSITE).

THE LIVING MOUNTAIN – FAUNA

Table Mountain est une réserve naturelle. On y trouvera des 'cone bushes' Leucadendron gandogeri (CI-CONTRE, EN HAUT À GAUCHE), des 'crassulas' Crassula coccinea (CI-CONTRE, EN HAUT À DROITE), des 'ericas' Erica cerinthoides (CI-CONTRE, EN BAS À GAUCHE), et des protéas Leucospermum cordifolium (CI-CONTRE, EN BAS À DROITE). Parmi la faune sur la montagne on pourra voir les charmants 'dassies' – rock hyrax (CI-DESSUS).

Der Tafelberg ist Schutzgebiet für eine farbenfreudige Vielfalt einheimischer Blütenpflanzen, wie die Leucadendron (GEGENÜBER OBEN LINKS), die Crassula oder Rote Fettpflanze, (GEGENÜBER OBEN RECHTS), Heidekrautpflanzen (GEGENÜBER UNTEN LINKS) und Nadelkissenproteen (GEGENÜBER UNTEN RECHTS). Die possierlichen Klippschliefer (OBEN) gehören zur Tierwelt auf dem Berg.

signal hill

18

THE FORESHORE

The view from Signal Hill reveals skyscrapers standing cheek by jowl on the Foreshore flanking Table Bay Harbour (ABOVE). Many of these buildings were built on an area reclaimed from the sea for urban development. Cape Town's Topless Bus stops on Signal Hill (OPPOSITE) to give tourists unhindered views of Table Mountain and the city bowl.

SIGNAL HILL VISTA

Vus de Signal Hill, les gratte-ciels se serrent sur le Foreshore adjacent au port dans Table Bay (CI-CONTRE). Un grand nombre de ces immeubles furent bâtis sur du terrain asséché, reconquis sur la mer. Le Topless Bus de Cape Town emmène les touristes au sommet de Signal Hill, leur donnant une vue ininterrompue de la ville et de Table Mountain (CI-DESSUS).

Vom Signalhügel aus gesehen, drängen sich die Hochhäuser auf der Foreshore um das Hafengebiet in der Tafelbucht (GEGENÜBER). Ein Großteil dieser Gebäude wurde auf dem Meer abgerungenen Boden (Foreshore bedeutet ‚Vor-der-Küste') errichtet. Der ‚Oben-ohne' Bus hält auf dem Signalhügel (OBEN) an, um den Touristen einen ungehinderten Blick auf den Tafelberg und den Stadtkern zu bieten.

LION'S HEAD

With the Twelve Apostles as his scenic backdrop, a paraglider heads skyward from the slopes of Lion's Head.

Un parapente prend son envol au départ de Lion's Head; au fond, les Twelve Apostles (douze apôtres).

Mit dem malerischen Panorama der Zwölf Apostel im Hintergrund, erhebt sich ein Gleitschirmflieger von den Hängen des Löwenkopfes aus in die Lüfte.

SIGNAL HILL SHRINE

The tomb or *kramat* of Muslim holy man Mohammed Gasan Gaibie Shah stands on top of the saddle linking Lion's Head and Signal Hill.

La tombe (*kramat*) du saint homme musulman Mohammed Gasan Gaibie Shah se trouve sur la crête qui relie Lion's Head à Signal Hill.

Grabmal des frommen Muslimen, Mohammed Gasan Gaibie Shah, auf dem Bergkamm zwischen Signalhügel und Löwenkopf.

CASTLE OF GOOD HOPE, AN EAGLE'S EYE VIEW

THE CASTLE

The pentagonal Castle of Good Hope (OPPOSITE), built during the 17th century, replaced the mud and clay fortress established by Commander Jan van Riebeeck in 1652. Today tourists pass through its portals (RIGHT) to view the dungeons and other relics of a bygone age.

Le fort de Bonne Espérance (Castle of Good Hope), bâti au 17ième, remplace la forteresse aux murs d'argile construite en 1652 par le commandant de l'époque, Jan van Riebeeck. De nos jours, les touristes viennent au fort (À DROITE) pour voir les oubliettes et autres reliques du passé.

Die fünfarmige Festung ‚Kastell der Guten Hoffnung' (GEGENÜBER), wurde im 17. Jahrhundert erbaut und ersetzte die Lehmfestung, die der Befehlshaber Jan van Riebeeck 1652 errichtete. Heute schlendern Touristen durch den Torbogen (RECHTS), um die Verliese und andere Relikte vergangener Zeiten zu besichtigen.

OLD WORLD ELEGANCE

The cobblestone courtyards within the Castle's walls flank the Dolphin Pool and fountain (ABOVE), while the elegant interiors display the priceless works of art by Dutch and British artists in the William Fehr Collection, and period pieces dating back to the 18th century (OPPOSITE).

WILLIAM FEHR COLLECTION

Abrités derrière les remparts dans la cour intérieure du fort, se trouvent le Dolphin Pool et sa fontaine (CI-CONTRE). A l'intérieur, dans les salles au décor élégant, on pourra admirer la William Fehr Collection ainsi que des antiquités remontant au 18ième (CI-DESSUS).

Das Delphinbecken und der Springbrunnen liegen im kopfstein-gepflasterten Innenhof der Festung (GEGENÜBER). In den eleganten Räumen werden die zur William-Fehr-Sammlung gehörenden prächtigen Gemälde holländischer und britischer Maler ausgestellt, sowie auch Kunstgegenstände des 18. Jahrhunderts (OBEN).

CITY HALL

The aroma of fried fish and flowers wafts through the stalls on the Grand Parade, which becomes a huge informal flea market on Wednesdays and Saturdays. Shoppers can browse among stalls selling second-hand books, antiques, bric-à-brac and bales of linen (ABOVE), displayed under the imposing façade of the City Hall. Bright, African-styled garments are touted by this street-trader (OPPOSITE).

GRAND PARADE VENDOR

Le fumet de poisson frit et l'arôme des fleurs coupées se propagent entre les étals de la Grand Parade, qui, le mercredi et le samedi, se transforme en un vaste marché aux puces. On y trouvera des vieux livres, des antiquités et du bric-à-brac, des rouleaux d'étoffes (CI-CONTRE) étalés au pied de la façade imposante de l'Hôtel de ville. Des vêtements ethniques sont offerts en vente par ces marchands de la Grand Parade (CI-DESSUS).

Der Duft von Bratfisch und Schnittblumen hängt zwischen den Ständen auf dem Paradeplatz, der sich mittwochs und samstags in einen riesigen Flohmarkt verwandelt. Käufer schlendern an den Ständen entlang, wo alte Bücher, Antiquitäten, Trödel und Stoffballen vor der imposanten Fassade des Rathauses ausgestellt sind (GEGENÜBER). Dieser Händler (OBEN) bietet farbenfreudige Kleidungsstücke mit afrikanischen Motiven an.

DISTRICT SIX MUSEUM

DISTRICT SIX MEMORABILIA

Haunting photographs and other artefacts in the District Six Museum on Buitenkant Street (OPPOSITE) commemorate the forced removal of 50,000 people and the destruction of their homes by the apartheid government in 1966. The museum houses all the original District Six street signs (BOTTOM RIGHT), and on the floor are signatures of those who lost their homes (TOP RIGHT).

Des anciennes photos et autres objets exposés au District Six Museum dans Buitekant Street (CI-CONTRE) commémorent l'expulsion en 1966 de ses 50,000 habitants par le gouvernement d'apartheid. Le musée possède toutes les plaques authentiques de noms de rues de l'ancien District Six (EN BAS À DROITE); par terre on pourra voir les signatures de ceux qui ont perdu leur demeure (EN HAUT À DROITE).

Erinnerungsträchtige Fotografien und andere Gegenstände im District Six (Bezirk Sechs) Museum (LINKS) in der Buitenkantstraße gedenken der Zwangsaussiedlung von 50,000 Menschen und der Vernichtung ihrer Heimstätten, die 1966 von der Apartheidregierung verfügt wurde. Im Museum sind die ursprünglichen Straßenschilder ausgestellt und den Boden zieren Namenszüge der Betroffenen (RECHTS).

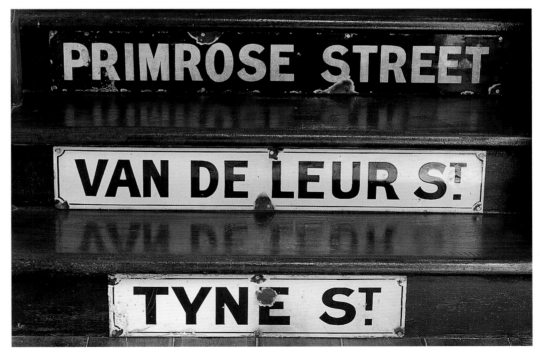

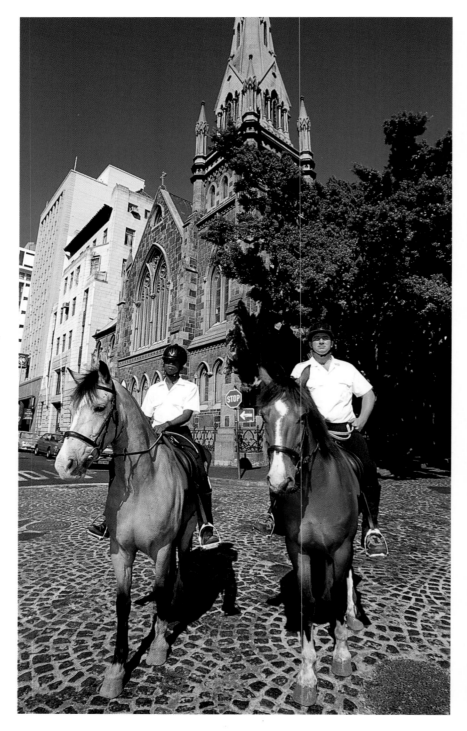

GREENMARKET SQUARE

A huddle of gaily coloured stalls (OPPOSITE RIGHT) provides a huge array of tantalising wares in central Cape Town's cobbled Greenmarket Square, where you can ask directions from mounted police (OPPOSITE LEFT) or have hair extensions added (RIGHT).

Greenmarket Square, dans le centre-ville, où se pressent de nombreux étals aux couleurs vives qui offrent un énorme choix de marchandises tentantes (CI-CONTRE À DROITE). On pourra y demander son chemin à la police montée (CI-CONTRE À GAUCHE) ou encore y acheter une perruque (À DROITE).

Auf dem kopfsteingepflasterten Greenmarket Square, im Herzen von Kapstadt, lockt die große Warenpalette der bunten, aneinander gedrängten Stände (GEGENÜBER RECHTS). Hier kann man auch die berittene Polizei um Auskunft bitten (GEGENÜBER LINKS) oder sich die Haare verlängern lassen (RECHTS).

ARTS AND CRAFTS

The exuberant colours and delicate ethnic crafts of Africa are a major draw-card for visitors to Greenmarket Square. Here you can get anything from masks and figurines (ABOVE) imported from as far afield as the Democratic Republic of the Congo, to bold local art (OPPOSITE).

GREENMARKET GALLERY

Les couleurs exubérantes et les délicats objets d'artisanat africain attirent de nombreux visiteurs à Greenmarket Square. Le choix est vaste, depuis les masques et figurines (CI-CONTRE) importés de la République démocratique du Congo aux ouvrages d'art étalés à même le pavé (CI-DESSUS).

Die leuchtenden Farben und die fein gearbeiteten ethnischen Handarbeiten bilden einen großen Anziehungspunkt für Besucher auf dem Greenmarket Square. Es gibt hier alles mögliche zu kaufen, von Masken und Figuren (GEGENÜBER) aus der fernen Demokratischen Republik des Kongos, bis zu den bunten, ausdrucksstarken Malereien von Straßenkünstlern, die auf der Straße ausgelegt sind (OBEN).

LONG STREET NIGHT LIFE

Late Victorian edifices, once the pride of Cape Town's shopping elite, today house bars and cafés in Long Street (ABOVE), more renowned for its junk shops and boarding houses than for its upmarket stores of yester-year. Central Cape Town is packed with informal outdoor eateries like this one (OPPOSITE).

EATING OUT

Long Street, avec ses maisons de style victorien, était autrefois un quartier chic de la ville. De nos jours, on y trouvera des bars et cafés (CI-CONTRE), ainsi que de nombreuses pensions voisinant des boutiques de bric-à-brac et autres vieilleries. Le centre-ville déborde de petits restaurants en plein air, comme celui-ci (CI-DESSUS).

Die eleganten Gebäude aus dem viktorianischen Zeitalter in der Long Street waren früher die Einkaufszeile verwöhnter Kapstädter. Heute findet man dort Kneipen und Imbißstuben (GEGENÜBER), und statt der noblen Geschäfte gibt es Ramschläden und Gasthäuser. Das Zentrum von Kapstadt hat eine große Anzahl dieserart Lokalitäten im Freien (OBEN).

BISTROS AND BROWSERS

Shoppers in central Cape Town take a break at one of the many outdoor bistros that line the pedestrian malls and thoroughfares (TOP RIGHT). Antiques and literary treasures can be found in Long and Church streets' second-hand shops (ABOVE RIGHT) and open-air stalls (ABOVE LEFT). The heady perfume of gaily coloured blooms (OPPOSITE) wafts through Adderley Street where flower sellers tout their fragrant harvest at very reasonable prices.

FLOWER MARKET

On n'a que l'embarras du choix entre les nombreux établissements en plein air dans le centre de Cape Town (CI-CONTRE, EN HAUT À DROITE). Les amateurs d'antiquités et de vieux livres fouinent dans les boutiques de Long et Church Street (CI-CONTRE, EN BAS À DROITE et CI-CONTRE, À GAUCHE). Le quartier d'Adderley Street est envahit par le parfum des fleurs aux couleurs éclatantes que les marchandes vendent à des prix raisonnables (CI-DESSUS).

Bistros in den Fußgängerzonen im Zentrum von Kapstadt laden ein zur Verschnaufpause (GEGENÜBER OBEN RECHTS). Antiquitäten und Literaturschätze gibt es beim Stöbern an Straßenständen und in Buchläden der Long Street (GEGENÜBER, LINKS und UNTEN RECHTS) zu entdecken. Der Wohlgeruch bunter Schnittblumen (OBEN) zieht durch die Adderley Street, wo Blumenhändler ihre duftende Ware zu erschwinglichen Preisen anbieten.

ST GEORGE'S MALL BUSKER

St George's Mall is a children's paradise, with buskers, bands, burger-stands and solo entertainers displaying their talents, like this balloon-maker (ABOVE) and dedicated artist (OPPOSITE). Shoppers can also browse among an array of goods displayed in stalls and on the ground.

STREET ARTIST

Le St George's Mall est un endroit favori des enfants, qui viennent y admirer les artistes et musiciens, comme cette créatrice de ballons (CI-CONTRE) et ce peintre (CI-DESSUS). On peut aussi y fouiner dans les nombreux étals et les marchandises exposées à même le pavé.

Die Fußgängerzone in der Stadtmitte, St. George's Mall, ist ein Paradies für Kinder, denn hier gibt es Imbißstände und Straßenmusikanten; auch Alleinunterhalter — wie dieser Ballonkünstler (GEGENÜBER) — und Straßenmaler (OBEN) führen ihre Talente vor. Ein vielfältiges Warenangebot, auf dem Boden und an Ständen ausgestellt, verlockt zum Anschauen und Kaufen.

ST GEORGE'S CATHEDRAL

ROSE WINDOW

St George's Anglican Cathedral (OPPOSITE) boasts the neo-Gothic influence of Herbert Baker and intricate stained glass (ABOVE).

La cathédrale anglicane St George (CI-CONTRE) aux vitraux complexes (CI-DESSUS), révèle le style de Herbert Baker.

Die anglikanische Kathedrale St. Georg (GEGENÜBER) im neugotischen Stil des Herbert Baker mit Kirchenglaskunstwerken (OBEN).

COMPANY GARDENS

The tree-lined avenues of the Company Gardens (ABOVE) invite strollers to relax on a park bench (OPPOSITE, TOP LEFT) and watch the squirrels (OPPOSITE, BOTTOM LEFT), or visit the South African National Gallery, with its imposing statue of former South African statesman Jan Smuts (OPPOSITE, RIGHT).

GRACIOUS GARDENS

Les avenues ombragées des Company Gardens (CI-CONTRE) attirent les promeneurs qui aiment s'y relaxer (CI-DESSUS, EN HAUT À GAUCHE) en observant les nombreux écureuils (CI-DESSUS, EN BAS À GAUCHE) ou encore de visiter la South African National Gallery, avec l'imposante statue de l'ancien homme d'Etat Jan Smuts (CI-DESSUS, À DROITE).

Die baumgesäumte Allee des Kompaniegartens (GEGENÜBER) verlockt die Fußgänger dazu, sich auf einer Parkbank zu entspannen und die Eichhörnchen zu beobachten (OBEN LINKS). Oder sie besuchen die Gemäldegalerie mit der imposanten Statue des südfrikanischen Staatsmannes Jan Smuts (OBEN RECHTS) davor.

SOUTH AFRICAN MUSEUM

The South African Museum in Cape Town's Gardens is a treasure-chest of South African memorabilia.

Le South African Museum dans les Company Gardens contient de nombreux objets d'intérêt historique, scientifique et artistique.

Das Südafrikanische Museum im Stadtpark von Kapstadt ist eine Schatztruhe südafrikanischer Erinnerungsstücke.

HOUSES OF PARLIAMENT

The columned entrance to the South African Houses of Parliament, whose portals have witnessed the profound political changes of the past 50 years.

La colonnade à l'entrée du Parlement sud-africain, dont les murs ont été témoins des importants changements politiques de ces 50 dernières années.

Das Säulenportal des südafrikanischen Parlamentsgebäudes ist ein Zeitzeuge der umwälzenden politischen Veränderungen der letzten 50 Jahre.

city centre

46

MOUNT NELSON GUARD

Five-star splendour awaits visitors to Cape Town's luxurious Mount Nelson Hotel (OPPOSITE) near the city centre, whose unmistakable colonial ambience is clearly reflected in its luxurious furnishings and the guards who stand watch over its entrance (LEFT).

Le faste de ses 5 étoiles attend les visiteurs au somptueux Mount Nelson Hotel (CI-CONTRE). Situé près du centre-ville, son ambiance coloniale distinctive est mise en évidence par l'ameublement luxueux et les gardes à l'entrée (À GAUCHE).

Fünf-Sterne-Pracht erwartet den Gast in Kapstadts luxuriösem Mount Nelson Hotel (GEGENÜBER), das in der Nähe des Stadtzentrums liegt. Die unverwechselbar koloniale Ambiente drückt sich in der eleganten Inneneinrichtung aus und auch in der Wache an der Einfahrt (LINKS).

MOUNT NELSON HOTEL

BO-KAAP HOUSES

Colourful Edwardian buildings (ABOVE) and delightful corner cafés (OPPOSITE) grace the Malay Quarter, or Bo-Kaap, on the lower slopes of Signal Hill. This area is home to some of Cape Town's large Muslim community.

ROSE CORNER CAFÉ

Le Malay Quarter, ou Bo-Kaap, est situé sur le versant de Signal Hill. On y verra de pittoresques maisons du style de l'époque d'Édouard VII (CI-CONTRE) et de plaisants cafés (CI-DESSUS). Le quartier est habité par une nombreuse population musulmane.

Bunt angestrichene Flachdachhäuser (GEGENÜBER) und urige Tante-Emma-Läden (OBEN) kennzeichnen das Malaienviertel, oder Bo-Kaap, an den unteren Hängen des Signalhügels. Hier lebt ein Teil der großen muslimischen Bevölkerung von Kapstadt.

TANA BARU CEMETERY

Revered graves of Holy Men of the Islamic faith who died in the Cape are accommodated in the Tana Baru Cemetery (ABOVE and OPPOSITE) at the top end of Longmarket Street. This cemetery is named after Imam Abdullah Kadi Abdus Salaam, better known as Tana Baru. There are over 20 recognised Muslim burial places or *kramats* in the Cape Peninsula.

TANA BARU TOMB

Le Tana Baru Cemetery, au bout de Longmarket Street, contient les tombes révérées de plusieurs saints hommes de la foi islamique qui décédèrent à Cape Town (CI-CONTRE et CI-DESSUS). Le cimetière est nommé d'après l'imam Abdullah Kadi Abdus Salaam, mieux connu sous le nom de Tana Baru. Il y a plus de 20 de ces cimetières musulmanes, ou *kramats*, dans la péninsule du Cap.

Die Gräber besonders frommer Muslimen, die am Kap verstorben sind, liegen im Tana Baru Friedhof (GEGENÜBER und OBEN) am oberen Ende der Longmarket Street und werden ehrfürchtig gepflegt. Der Friedhof ist benannt nach dem Imam Abdullah Kadi Abdus Salaam, besser bekannt als Tana Baru. Es gibt mehr als 20 anerkannte Grabstätten oder Kramats auf der Kaphalbinsel.

CAPE MINSTRELS

Cape Town rocks to the sounds of Dixie bands on 'Tweede Nuwe Jaar'
('Second New Year' – 2nd of January) during the 'Coon Carnival' when
thousands of gaily dressed minstrels (ABOVE) march through the city's streets.
Some revellers, such as this kettle-blower (OPPOSITE), rely on ingenious
musical improvisations to produce their festive sounds.

NEW YEAR CARNIVAL

Cape Town danse durant le 'Coon Carnival', quand des milliers de 'minstrels', portant des costumes aux couleurs criardes (CI-CONTRE) marchent dans la cité pour célébrer le 'Tweede Nuwe Jaar' (deuxième nouvel an). Certains des participants, comme ce 'joueur de bouilloire' (CI-DESSUS), inventent leurs propres instruments pour produire des sons originaux.

Am sogenannte 'Zweiten Neujahrstag' (2. Januar) erklingt in Kapstadt die Musik der Dixie-Kapellen, die den Coon Carnival begehen. Tausende bunt ausstaffierte Musikanten (GEGENÜBER) ziehen durch die Straßen der Stadt. Einige der Umzugsteilnehmer, wie etwa dieser Kesselbläser (OBEN), entlocken ihren eigenwilligen Musikinstrumenten festliche Klänge.

CAPE ARGUS CYCLE TOUR

Cape Town's premier sporting event, the Cape Argus Pick 'n Pay Cycle Tour, attracts tens of thousands of cyclists, who set out from central Cape Town at first light (LEFT) to complete the gruelling 104-kilometre course in summer. An event of equal stature is the 56-kilometre Two Oceans Marathon (OPPOSITE), which attracts runners from all over the world.

TWO OCEANS MARATHON

L'événement sportif le plus important de Cape Town, le Cape Argus Pick 'n Pay Cycle Tour, attire des dizaines de milliers de cyclistes chaque été. La course prend son départ à l'aube dans le centre-ville (CI-CONTRE); le parcours, qui est exténuant, est long de 104 kilomètres. Un autre événement d'importance semblable, et qui attire des participants du monde entier, est le Two Oceans Marathon (CI-DESSUS); son parcours est de 56 kilomètres.

Das größte alljährliche Sportereignis in Kapstadt, das Cape Argus-Pick 'n Pay-Fahrradrennen, lockt Zehntausende von Teilnehmern, die im sommerlichen Morgengrauen losradeln (GEGENÜBER), um die strapaziöse Strecke von 104 Kilometern zu bewältigen. Ebenso bedeutend ist der Two-Oceans-Marathonlauf (OBEN) über 56 Kilometer, an dem Langstreckenläufer aus aller Welt teilnehmen.

V&A WATERFRONT

Framed by Table Mountain in the background, the main promenade at Cape Town's Victoria and Alfred Waterfront serves as a jetty for yachts and cruisers (ABOVE) which take visitors on pleasure trips to Robben Island and around Table Bay. Informal concerts, such as this one by Cape Minstrels at the Waterfront's Amphitheatre (OPPOSITE), attract appreciative audiences.

AMPHITHEATRE ARTISTES

La promenade principale du Victoria et Alfred Waterfront, où sont amarrés les yachts et autres embarcations qui emmènent les visiteurs à Robben Island ou en excursion dans Table Bay (CI-CONTRE). Des concerts impromptus, comme celui-ci avec les Cape Minstrels (CI-DESSUS) au Waterfront Amphitheatre, attirent un nombreux public.

Mit dem Tafelberg als Hintergrund, bietet die Hauptpromenade in der Victoria und Alfred Waterfront Anlegestellen für Jachten und Ausflugsschiffe, die Überfahrten nach Robbeneiland und Hafenrundfahrten in der Tafelbucht anbieten (GEGENÜBER). Freilichtkonzerte wie dieses, wo eine Kapstädter Musikantentruppe im Amphitheater an der Waterfront auftritt (OBEN), locken immer ein dankbares Publikum.

WATERFRONT REFLECTIONS

The dazzling lights of the Waterfront's Victoria Wharf shopping centre (ABOVE) weave their own magic in the waters of Table Bay Harbour, while the Hildebrand Restaurant nearby (OPPOSITE) rewards patrons with mouthwatering seafood cuisine and congenial surroundings.

ALFRESCO DINING

Les lumières éclatantes du centre commercial Victoria Wharf au Waterfront (CI-CONTRE) illuminent les eaux du port comme par magie. Dans l'ambiance sympathique du restaurant Hildebrand (CI-DESSUS), les clients se régalent de délicieux fruits de mer.

Die funkelnden Lichter des Victoria Wharf Einkaufszentrums an der Waterfront (GEGENÜBER) malen eine Spiegellandschaft auf dem Wasser des Hafenbeckens, während das nahegelegene Hildebrand Restaurant (OBEN) die Gäste mit delikaten Meeresfrüchten und einer traumhaften Atmosphäre verwöhnt.

SHOPPERS' PARADISE

QUAYSIDE CHARM

The Waterfront's irresistible charm is evident in its spacious interiors (OPPOSITE) and charming dockside ambience (ABOVE).

Le charme irrésistible du Waterfront est mis en valeur par les vastes intérieurs (CI-CONTRE) et l'atmosphère charmante de ses quais (CI-DESSUS).

Der Charme der Waterfront offenbart sich in den großzügigen Passagen (GEGENÜBER) und malerischen Hafenanlagen (OBEN).

TWO OCEANS AQUARIUM

Young visitors to the Waterfront's Two Oceans Aquarium are mesmerised by a shoal of yellowtail cruising past in the crystalline depths of the main tank.

Un banc de poisson dans les eaux cristallines du Two Oceans Aquarium au Waterfront, fascine des jeunes visiteurs.

Zwei jugendliche Besucher im Two Oceans Aquarium beobachten fasziniert, wie ein Schwarm Gelbschwänze in der kristallklaren Tiefe des großen Fischtanks vorüberzieht.

AQUATIC ATTRACTIONS

Tourists pause to examine the sea-life of some of the Aquarium's smaller display tanks.

Les touristes observent avec grand intérêt la vie marine exposée à l'Aquarium.

Besucher verweilen vor den kleineren Fischtanks im Aquarium, um das Meeresleben hinter Glas zu studieren.

TABLE BAY HOTEL

A concierge waits to welcome guests to the five-star luxury of the Waterfront's
Table Bay Hotel (ABOVE). Nearby, seafarers may board the *Spirit of Victoria*
(OPPOSITE) for scenic cruises around the bay.

SPIRIT OF VICTORIA

Le portier du Table Bay Hotel, un établissement de grand luxe au Waterfront, est prêt à accueillir les clients à leur arrivée (CI-CONTRE). Un peu plus loin, les amateurs de voile vont en excursion dans la baie à bord du *Spirit of Victoria* (CI-DESSUS).

Ein Portier wartet darauf, die Gäste des Fünf-Sterne-Luxushotels, Table Bay, an der Waterfront zu begrüßen (GEGENÜBER). Nicht weit entfernt, können Segelbegeisterte an Bord der *Spirit of Victoria* gehen, um eine kleine Kreuzfahrt um die Bucht zu unternehmen (OBEN).

ROBBEN ISLAND AERIAL

Cut off from the mainland by the icy waters of the Atlantic Ocean, Robben Island (LEFT) served as a prison home to South Africa's most celebrated politician, former president Nelson Mandela, for some 18 years. From watchtowers (OPPOSITE LEFT) on the island prison guards kept up a 24-hour surveillance of inmates, who were locked up at night in cells like this one (OPPOSITE RIGHT).

ISLAND PRISON

Robben Island (CI-CONTRE), séparée du continent par les eaux glaciales de l'Atlantique, fut pendant 18 ans la résidence forcée du plus célèbre politicien sud-africain, Nelson Mandela. Un des miradors d'où les gardes surveillaient le pénitencier de l'île 24 heures sur 24 (CI-DESSUS À GAUCHE). La nuit, les prisonniers étaient enfermés dans des cellules comme celle-ci (CI-DESSUS À DROITE).

Vom Festland durch die eisigen Fluten des Atlantik abgeschnitten, bildete Robbeneiland (GEGENÜBER) für 18 Jahre das Gefängnisheim des berühmtesten Inhaftierten Südafrikas, Nelson Mandela. Einer der Wachttürme (OBEN LINKS), die rundum die Uhr die Gefangenen bewachten, die nachts in Zellen wie dieser (OBEN RECHTS) eingeschlossen wurden.

GOVERNOR'S RESIDENCE

Robben Island's first governor lived in this house (ABOVE) which, unlike the
island prison, had unhindered access to the scenic beauty of the Atlantic and
Table Mountain in the distance (OPPOSITE). The island is also a conservation
area, providing sanctuary to a number of bird species, mammals and reptiles.

BIRDWATCHING PARADISE

Le premier gouverneur de Robben Island vivait dans cette maison (CI-CONTRE). A la différence du pénitencier de l'île, la vue de la maison vers Table Mountain et l'océan Atlantique n'est aucunement limitée (CI-DESSUS). L'île est aussi une zone de conservation, abritant de nombreuses espèces d'oiseaux, de reptiles et de mammifères.

Der erste Gouverneur wohnte in diesem Haus auf Robbeneiland (GEGENÜBER), das – im Gegensatz zu dem Gefängnis – einen ungehinderten Blick auf den Atlantik und den Tafelberg im Hintergrund hatte (OBEN). Die Insel bildet auch ein Naturschutzgebiet für verschiedene Vogelarten, Säugetiere und Reptilien.

MOUILLE POINT DUSK

Sunset over Mouille Point with Lion's Head in the background (ABOVE). After dark it's party time in Green Point as dozens of discos and restaurants, like the News Café (OPPOSITE), open their doors to revellers.

PARTY TIME

Coucher de soleil à Mouille Point avec Lion's Head à l'arrière plan (CI-CONTRE). Une fois la nuit tombée, Green Point s'anime, et les discos et restaurants, comme le News Café (CI-DESSUS) sont prêts à accueillir la clientèle.

Sonnenuntergang in Mouille Point; im Hintergrund der Löwenkopf (GEGENÜBER). Wenn es dunkel wird, bricht die gesellige Zeit an in Green Point, wo Dutzende von Discos und Restaurants, wie das News Café (OBEN), Unterhaltungssuchenden ihre Türen öffnen.

SEA POINT PROMENADE

Terraces, playparks and cobblestone boulevards line the seafront at Sea Point (ABOVE), Cape Town's premier seaside playground. In summer Sea Point's main attraction is the public pool on the edge of the Atlantic (OPPOSITE).

SEA POINT SWIMMING POOL

Le front de mer à Sea Point, très populaire parmi les habitants de Cape Town, est bordé par un boulevard, des terrasses et des terrains de jeux (CI-CONTRE). Durant l'été, l'attraction principale est la piscine publique au bord de l'Atlantique (CI-DESSUS).

Terrassen, Spielplätze und gepflasterte Boulevards säumen die Küstenstraße in Sea Point (GEGENÜBER), Kapstadts bekanntestem Vergnügungsviertel am Meer. Im Sommer ist das öffentliche Schwimmbad am Atlantik die Hauptattraktion (OBEN).

clifton

THE CAPE RIVIERA

Lying between imposing mountains and the sea, Clifton's four beaches (ABOVE) are regarded as the Riviera of the south-western Cape – a mecca for bronzed bodies soaking in the sun on the idyllic sands (OPPOSITE).

CLIFTON'S FOURTH BEACH

Nichées entre les montagnes et la mer, les quatre plages de Clifton (CI-CONTRE) sont considérées comme étant la Riviera du Cap, une Mecque pour les amateurs de bronzage qui envahissent ses sables idylliques pendant l'été (CI-DESSUS).

Die vier Strände von Clifton (GEGENÜBER) liegen zwischen der imposanten Gebirgskette und dem Meer und gelten als Riviera am südwestlichen Kap – ein Mekka für die gebräunten Körper, die sich auf den idyllischen Sandstränden in der Sonne aalen (OBEN).

TWELVE APOSTLES

CAMPS BAY

The Twelve Apostles loom above Camps Bay and its long beach (OPPOSITE), where beachgoers revel in the sun (ABOVE).

Les 'Twelve Apostles' dominent Camps Bay et sa longue plage (CI-CONTRE), où les estivants se délectent au soleil (CI-DESSUS).

Die Zwölf Apostel erheben sich hinter dem Strand von Camps Bay (GEGENÜBER), wo man sich in der Sonne amüsiert (OBEN).

BEACH GAMES

Crowds flock to the seaside at Camps Bay during the long hot summers for a
game of volleyball on the beach (ABOVE), or to sample the culinary delights of
the suburb's variety of restaurants (OPPOSITE).

TRENDY EATERIES

Les vacanciers affluent sur le front de mer à Camps Bay; on y joue au volley-ball sur la plage (CI-CONTRE), ou on goûte les délices gastronomiques dans les nombreux restaurants de l'endroit (CI-DESSUS).

Die Scharen strömen in den langen heißen Sommermonaten an den Strand von Camps Bay. Sie spielen Volleyball am Strand (GEGENÜBER) oder genießen die kulinarischen Genüsse der vielen unterschiedlichen Restaurants (OBEN) mit Ausblick aufs Meer.

atlantic seaboard

80

COASTAL SPLENDOUR

Lion's Head and the Twelve Apostles form an imposing backdrop to the
sinuous curves of the coastline between Sea Point and Hout Bay (ABOVE).
Near Llandudno, on the way to Hout Bay, streetside vendors display an array
of exotic shells and local crafts (OPPOSITE).

ROADSIDE VENDORS

Avec la vue spectaculaire de Lion's Head et des Twelve Apostles dans l'arrière-plan, la route serpente le long de la côte entre Sea Point et Hout Bay (CI-CONTRE). Près de Llandudno, des coquillages exotiques et des objets d'artisanat local sont offerts en vente (CI-DESSUS).

Der Löwenkopf und die Zwölf Apostel bilden eine imposante Kulisse für den Küstenstreifen, der sich zwischen Sea Point und Hout Bay dahinwindet (GEGENÜBER). Bei Llandudno, auf dem Wege nach Hout Bay, bieten Händler exotische Muscheln und einheimische Handarbeiten feil (OBEN).

SEAL CRUISE

A close encounter with the seals of Duiker Island, a short boat ride from Hout Bay Harbour, enthralls visitors (ABOVE). On their return to the harbour they're welcomed by a cheerful ensemble of Cape Minstrels with their unique brand of Dixie music (OPPOSITE).

DOCKSIDE MINSTRELS

Située à peu de distance de Hout Bay, Duiker Island captive les visiteurs par sa population de phoques (CI-CONTRE). A leur retour au port, les touristes sont accueillis par la joviale troupe des Cape Minstrels et leur unique style musical Dixie (CI-DESSUS).

Eine Begegnung mit den Seehunden auf Duiker Island erfordert nur eine kurze Bootsfahrt von Hout Bay und begeistert die Besucher (GEGENÜBER). Bei der Rückkehr im Hafen werden sie von einer kleinen Gruppe Musikanten empfangen, die ihre eigenwillige Dixiemusik spielen (OBEN).

HOUT BAY BEACHFRONT

Patrons of Hout Bay's Dunes Restaurant relax in the sun (ABOVE), a stone's throw away from the beach. Hout Bay harbour, with its fleets of gaily coloured trawlers (OPPOSITE) and mountain landscapes in the distance, is one of Cape Town's premier tourist attractions.

HOUT BAY HARBOUR

A deux pas de la plage de Hout Bay, les clients de Dunes Restaurant se relaxent au soleil (CI-CONTRE). Entouré de montagnes, le port de Hout Bay, avec ses nombreux chalutiers aux couleurs vives (CI-DESSUS), est une des principales attractions touristiques de Cape Town.

Gäste des Dunes Restaurant in Hout Bay entspannen sich nur einen Katzensprung vom Strand entfernt in der Sonne (GEGENÜBER). Der Hafen von Hout Bay mit seiner Flotte grell bemalter Fischerboote und der Bergkulisse im Hintergrund (OBEN), ist eine der größten Touristenattraktionen von Kapstadt.

LONG BEACH

HORSEBACK RIDING, LONG BEACH

The soft white sands of Noordhoek's Long Beach (OPPOSITE) bring equestrians out for a ride along the water's edge (ABOVE).

Les sables de Long Beach à Noordhoek (CI-CONTRE) attirent les amateurs d'équitation qui s'y promènent au bord de l'eau (CI-DESSUS).

Der weiche weiße Sand am Strand von Long Beach in Noordhoek (GEGENÜBER) verlockt zu einem Ausritt am Meer (OBEN).

CAPE OF GOOD HOPE NATURE RESERVE

The Cape of Good Hope Nature Reserve (ABOVE) marks the end of the long peninsula on which Cape Town's southern and western suburbs are built. The old lighthouse at its tip (OPPOSITE LEFT) used to warn mariners of treacherous seas and hidden reefs, while the Vasco Da Gama monument (OPPOSITE RIGHT) honours the memory of a great explorer.

CAPE POINT LANDMARKS

La réserve naturelle Cape of Good Hope Nature Reserve (CI-CONTRE) est située à l'extrémité de la longue péninsule loin des faubourgs de Cape Town. L'ancien phare de Cape Point (CI-DESSUS À GAUCHE) mettait en garde contre les mers dangereuses et la menace des récifs invisibles. Le monument Vasco Da Gama (CI-DESSUS À DROITE) commémore le grand explorateur.

Am Ende der langen Halbinsel, auf der sich die südlichen und westlichen Vororte Kapstadts ausbreiten, liegt das Naturschutzgebiet Kap der Guten Hoffnung (GEGENÜBER). Das Blinklicht des alten Leuchtturms (OBEN RECHTS) warnte früher die Seefahrer vor dem tückischen Meer und verborgenen Felsenriffen. Eine Kreuzsäule (OBEN LINKS) ehrt den großen Entdeckungsreisenden, Vasco da Gama.

THE CAPE OF GOOD HOPE

Attractions at the Cape of Good Hope Nature Reserve include a mountainside restaurant (OPPOSITE LEFT), a funicular which runs visitors to the top of Cape Point (OPPOSITE, TOP RIGHT), and the wreck of the *Thomas T Tucker* (OPPOSITE, BOTTOM RIGHT). The signpost (ABOVE) in the reserve announces the south-westernmost point of Africa.

CAPE POINT COLLAGE

Parmi les attractions de Cape of Good Hope Nature Reserve on trouvera un restaurant sur le flanc de la montagne (CI-DESSUS À GAUCHE), un funiculaire qui transporte les visiteurs au sommet de Cape Point (CI-DESSUS, EN HAUT À DROITE), et l'épave du *Thomas T Tucker* (CI-DESSUS, EN BAS À DROITE). Le panneau indicateur dans Cape of Good Hope Nature Reserve marque la position géographique de Cape Point (CI-CONTRE).

Anlaufpunkte im Naturschutzgebiet am Kap der Guten Hoffnung sind das Restaurant am Felshang (OBEN LINKS) und das Wrack der *Thomas T Tucker* (OBEN RECHTS). Man kann zwar auch hinauflaufen, aber weniger Energiegeladene ziehen eine Fahrt mit der Bergbahn auf die oberste Spitze vor (GANZ OBEN RECHTS). Eine Tafel verkündet, daß man sich hier am südwestlichsten Punkt des afrikanischen Kontinents befindet (GEGENÜBER).

BOULDERS BOARDWALK

Jackass (or African) penguins, so named for their donkey-like bray, are protected at Boulders (OPPOSITE), a small, scenic beach near Simon's Town. Because they are on the list of endangered species, visitors come from far to see them. Access is from the road above the beach via boardwalk (ABOVE).

PENGUINS AT BOULDERS

Les manchots d'Afrique, dont le cri ressemble au braiment de l'âne, sont protégés à Boulders (CI-DESSUS), une jolie petite plage près de Simon's Town. Les visiteurs viennent de loin pour observer ces animaux dont l'espèce est menacée. On accède à la plage par la route qui la longe, par un chemin de planches (CI-CONTRE).

Brillenpinguine (afrikanische Pinguine) haben einen Zufluchtsort gefunden bei Boulders (OBEN), einem kleinen, malerischen Strand bei Simon's Town. Besucher aus dem ganzen Land und von Übersee kommen hierher, um diese bedrohte Vogelart aus der Nähe zu sehen. Von der Straße oberhalb des Strandes gelangt man zu den Stellagen (GEGENÜBER).

SIMON'S TOWN HARBOUR

SIMON'S TOWN WATERFRONT

A beautiful natural harbour at Simon's Town (OPPOSITE) is the perfect setting for restaurants and small pleasure boats (ABOVE).

Simon's Town possède un beau port naturel (CI-CONTRE), cadre idéal pour les restaurants et les bateaux de plaisance (CI-DESSUS).

Der natürliche Hafen bei Simon's Town (GEGENÜBER) ist ein idealer Platz für Restaurants und Ausflugsboote (OBEN).

HISTORIC MAIN ROAD

The British colonial influence on Simon's Town is apparent in the quaint old Victorian-style buildings that flank the main road that runs through it (ABOVE). Attractions on the way include delicacies fresh from the sea (OPPOSITE LEFT) and a bronze statue, honouring a legendary old sea dog called Just Nuisance (OPPOSITE RIGHT), in Jubilee Square.

SIMON'S TOWN ATTRACTIONS

L'influence du style colonial britannique est en évidence dans les pittoresques maisons victoriennes qui bordent la rue principale de Simon's Town (CI-CONTRE). On y trouvera des restaurants spécialisés en fruits de mer (CI-DESSUS À GAUCHE) et dans Jubilee Square, la statue commémorant Just Nuisance, la légendaire mascotte de la marine (CI-DESSUS À DROITE).

Der Einfluß der britischen Kolonialzeit in Simon's Town fällt sofort ins Auge durch die malerischen, alten Gebäude im viktorianischen Stil, die an der Hauptstraße stehen (GEGENÜBER). Es gibt verschiedene Attraktionen, wie Delikates frisch aus dem Meer (OBEN LINKS) und eine Bronzestatue auf dem Jubilee Square, die zu Ehren eines legendären Hundes, der Just Nuisance (Bloß Blödsinn) hieß, errichtet wurde (OBEN RECHTS).

FISH HOEK BEACH

THE FAMILY BEACH

Warm water and gently sloping sands lure hobie-cat enthusiasts (OPPOSITE) and fun seekers (ABOVE) to Fish Hoek beach.

Les eaux tièdes de Fish Hoek attirent les amateurs de catamaran (CI-CONTRE), et les estivants avides de jeux de plage (CI-DESSUS).

Hobie-Cat-Segler (GEGENÜBER) und Strandgänger (OBEN) genießen das warme Wasser und den Sandstrand bei Fish Hoek.

KALK BAY PANORAMA

The old fishing harbour of Kalk Bay (ABOVE) overlooks an azure sea and distant mountains leading towards Cape Point. The harbour is a concourse for dozens of fishing boats (OPPOSITE) which harvest the nutrient-rich waters of the Atlantic for species such as hake, longfin and yellowfin tuna and snoek.

CATCH OF THE DAY, KALK BAY

Le vieux port de pêche de Kalk Bay (CI-CONTRE) est baigné par une mer d'azur, avec au fond, les montagnes dans la direction de Cape Point. C'est d'ici que des douzaines de bateaux de pêche (CI-DESSUS) partent pour sillonner les eaux riches en subsistance de l'Atlantique à la recherche de merlu, de thon et de barracuda (snoek).

Der alte Fischerhafen von Kalk Bay (GEGENÜBER) blickt über das blaue Meer zu den fernen Bergen, die sich bis zur Kapspitze entlangziehen. Der Hafen ist Drehscheibe für Dutzende von Fischerbooten (OBEN), die in den nährstoffreichen Gewässern des Atlantiks reiche Ernte halten. Beliebte Fischarten sind Seehecht, Thunfisch und Atun (Snoek).

SHOPPERS' DELIGHT

The back streets and byways of Kalk Bay's shopping district are a treasure trove of fascinating wares, from antiques, arts and crafts to kitchenware, such as that of the Cook's Room on display in a narrow walkway (ABOVE). Beads, basketware and other African crafts are favoured by tourists who pop into Kalk Bay's Cape to Cairo and Induna Village curio shops (OPPOSITE).

KALK BAY CRAFTS

Les ruelles et allées du quartier commercial de Kalk Bay où le visiteur trouvera des antiquaires, galeries d'art, magasins de souvenirs et d'objets d'artisanat, ou encore du bric-à-brac d'ustensiles de cuisine, comme chez 'Cook's Room' qui expose dans cette allée étroite (CI-CONTRE). Ornements perlés, vannerie et autres objets d'artisanat Africain sont en vente au maga- sin de souvenirs Cape to Cairo and Induna Village (CI-DESSUS et À DROITE).

Abgelegene Gäßchen in dem Einkaufszentrum von Kalk Bay, das eine wahre Schatztruhe faszinierender Waren ist, von Antiquitäten, Kunst- gegenständen und Handarbeiten, bis zu Küchenartikeln, wie jene im ‚Reich der Köche', (GEGENÜBER). Perlen, Korbarbeiten und andere afrikanische Handarbeiten sind begehrt bei den Touristen, die es in Kalk Bay in die Läden ‚Cape to Cairo' und ‚Induna Village' zieht (OBEN und RECHTS).

ST JAMES BEACH

Clear skies bring out the colours of bathing huts on the beachfront at
St James (ABOVE) and a flotilla of kites at nearby Muizenberg (OPPOSITE).

MUIZENBERG MAGIC

Les couleurs vives des cabines de bain à St James (CI-CONTRE) et de cette armada de cerfs-volants à Muizenberg, la plage voisine (CI-DESSUS), contrastent merveilleusement avec le bleu du ciel.

Der strahlend blaue Himmel hebt das Bunt der Badehäuschen am Strand von St James (GEGENÜBER) und der fantasievollen Drachen im nahegelegenen Muizenberg (OBEN) hervor.

RONDEVLEI WETLAND

More than 200 species of bird, many of them wetland species such as pelicans (OPPOSITE), inhabit Rondevlei Bird Sanctuary near Muizenberg. Hides positioned among the reeds (ABOVE) enable visitors to photograph the inhabitants of this avian wonderland at close quarters.

WATERBIRD WONDERLAND

Plus de 200 espèces d'oiseaux, dont de nombreuses variétés aquatiques, comme ces pélicans (CI-DESSUS), vivent dans la réserve du Rondevlei Bird Sanctuary près de Muizenberg. Des postes d'observation situés dans les roseaux (CI-CONTRE) permettent aux visiteurs de photographier les oiseaux de près.

Mehr als 200 Vogelarten, viele davon Wasservögel, wie etwa die Pelikane (OBEN), bevölkern das Rondevlei Vogelschutzgebiet bei Muizenberg. Verstecke zur Vogelbeobachtung (GEGENÜBER) sind im Schilf aufgestellt und ermöglichen Besuchern, die Bewohner dieses Vogelparadieses aus nächster Nähe zu fotografieren.

CONSTANTIA VALLEY

PASTORAL SCENES

Fertile vineyards (OPPOSITE) and Cosmos blooms (ABOVE) bring contrasting colours to the undulating farmlands of Constantia.

Les couleurs pastel des fleurs sauvages (CI-DESSUS) et les vignobles (CI-CONTRE) sont caractéristiques de la vallée de Constantia.

Weinberge (GEGENÜBER) und Kosmosblüten (OBEN) bringen Farbkontraste in das hügelige Landwirtschaftsgebiet von Constantia.

GROOT CONSTANTIA ESTATE

This gracious image (ABOVE) perfectly illustrates the elegance and rustic grandeur of the Cape Dutch architecture at Groot Constantia Estate, where visitors relax for lunch under the trees at the Tavern Restaurant (OPPOSITE).

TALK AT THE TAVERN

Le caractère grandiose et l'élégance du style hollandais du Cap sont parfaitement mis en évidence dans l'architecture du manoir au domaine de Groot Constantia (CI-CONTRE). Les visiteurs peuvent s'y relaxer et déjeuner à l'ombre des arbres au restaurant 'The Tavern' (CI-DESSUS).

Das Herrenhaus mit dem schönen Giebel (GEGENÜBER) vermittelt die anmutige Eleganz und ländliche Großzügigkeit des kapholländischen Baustils auf dem Groot Constantia Anwesen. Hier können Besucher sich beim Mittagessen in der ‚Taverne' (OBEN) unter den Bäumen entspannen.

KIRSTENBOSCH NATIONAL BOTANICAL GARDEN

BLOOMS AND BUTTRESSES

Kirstenbosch National Botanical Garden (OPPOSITE) attracts thousands of nature-lovers to its rolling terraces, verdant lawns and breathtaking displays of indigenous flowers (RIGHT).

Le jardin botanique de Kirstenbosch (CI-CONTRE), avec ses vertes pelouses ondulantes et ses splendides collections de fleurs indigènes (À DROITE), attire des milliers d'amoureux de la nature.

Der Nationale Botanische Garten von Kirstenbosch (GEGENÜBER) lockt Tausende von Naturliebhabern mit seinen ausgedehnten Anlagen, den grünen Rasenflächen und der atemberaubenden, bunten Vielfalt der einheimischen Wildblumen (RECHTS).

GARDEN SYMPHONY

The skies above Kirstenbosch National Botanical Garden come alive with colours and lights when fireworks displays (OPPOSITE) celebrate the end of the popular New Year concert (ABOVE).

KIRSTENBOSCH CELEBRATIONS

Les cieux au-dessus de Kirstenbosch éclatent dans une explosion de lumière et de couleurs (CI-DESSUS) quand les feux d'artifice annoncent la fin du populaire concert de Nouvel An (CI-CONTRE).

Der Himmel über Kirstenbosch funkelt und schillert in einem Kaleidoskop von Licht und Farbe während einer Feuerwerksveranstaltung (OBEN), die den Abschluß des beliebten Neujahrskonzertes bildet (GEGENÜBER).

BAXTER THEATRE

The Baxter Theatre (ABOVE) in Rondebosch is one of Cape Town's most popular entertaiment venues. The interior of Josephine's Mill (OPPOSITE) in Newlands, built in 1840 and named after the Crown Princess of Sweden, still houses the machinery of the original working mill.

JOSEPHINE'S MILL

Le Baxter Theatre (CI-CONTRE) à Rondebosch est un des plus populaires de Cape Town. Une vue de l'intérieur de Josephine's Mill (CI-DESSUS) à Newlands. Ce moulin à eau, construit en 1840, est nommé d'après la princesse héritière de Suède, et contient toujours la machinerie originelle.

Das Baxter Theater (GEGENÜBER) in Rondebosch ist eine der beliebtesten Unterhaltungsstätten in Kapstadt. In der Josphinenmühle (OBEN), die 1840 gebaut und nach der Kronprinzessin von Schweden benannt wurde, stehen noch die alten Anlagen der ursprünglichen Mühle.

NEWLANDS CRICKET GROUND

For decades the roars of appreciative crowds have boomed through the stands of the Newlands cricket ground (ABOVE) and Newlands rugby ground (OPPOSITE), scene of some of the world's greatest sporting contests.

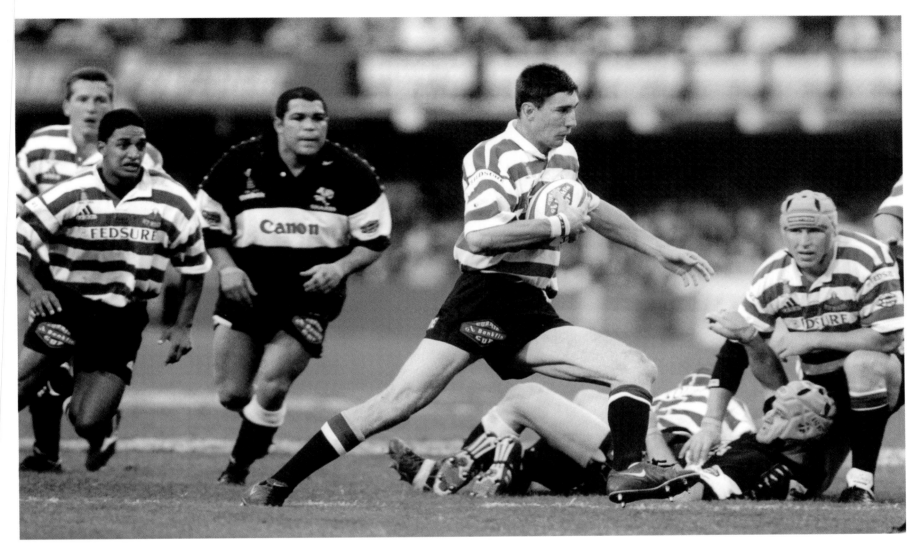

RUGBY FEVER, NEWLANDS

Pendant des décennies les acclamations enthousiastes des foules de spectateurs ont fait vibrer les tribunes des terrains de cricket (CI-CONTRE) et de rugby (CI-DESSUS), à Newlands, théâtre d'événements sportifs d'importance mondiale.

Die lautstarke Begeisterung der Scharen hallt seit Jahrzehnten in Newlands über den Criketplatz (GEGENÜBER) und das Rugbyfeld (OBEN). Hier wurden schon viele Weltspiele ausgetragen.

KENILWORTH'S J & B MET

One of the premier events on Cape Town's racing calendar is the J & B Metropolitan Handicap at Kenilworth Race Course (ABOVE). Dedicated followers of fashion get as much attention as the horses at the Met, and the winners of the fashion stakes (OPPOSITE) always parade their outfits for the cameras.

J & B STYLE

Un des plus importants événement de la saison des courses à Cape Town est le J & B Metropolitan Handicap au champ de courses de Kenilworth (CI-CONTRE). Ceux qui suivent la mode de près reçoivent tout autant d'attention que les chevaux, et les gagnants des concours d'élégance paradent toujours leur toilette pour les photographes (CI-DESSUS).

Unter den Pferderennen, die in Kapstadt regelmäßig abgehalten werden, nimmt das J & B Metropolitan Handicap auf der Rennbahn in Kenilworth (GEGENÜBER) eine Vorrangstellung ein. Dabei genießen die modebewußten Zuschauer die Aufmerksamkeit des Publikums im gleichen Maße wie die Pferde. Sie werden ebenfalls preisgekrönt (OBEN) und stellen sich gerne den Fotografen.

RHODES MEMORIAL

Morning sun illuminates the stately steps and columns of Rhodes Memorial on the slopes of Table Mountain.

Le soleil levant illumine l'imposant monument de Rhodes Memorial, érigé sur les flancs de Table Mountain.

Am Hang der Teufelsspitze steht das imposante Rhodes Denkmal. Das Licht der Morgensonne beleuchtet Stufen und Säulen.

MOSTERT'S MILL

South Africa's only operating mill, Mostert's Mill, was built in 1796 after the Battle of Muizenberg in the valley of the Liesbeek River. Today it can be seen just off De Waal Drive, an historic monument to the early days of the Cape.

Mostert Mill, en bordure de De Waal drive, est un monument historique. Construit en 1796, après la bataille de Muizenberg dans la vallée de la Liesbeek River, il est le seul moulin à vent en fonctionnement en Afrique du Sud.

Südafrikas einzige funktionsfähige Mühle, Mosterts Mühle, wurde 1796 nach der Schlacht von Muizenberg im Tal des Liesbeekflußes errichtet. Als ein historisches Monument, das an die alte Zeit am Kap erinnert, sieht man es heute neben der Schnellstraße De Waal Drive.

UNIVERSITY OF CAPE TOWN

An aerial view of one of South Africa's most revered institutions, the University of Cape Town on the slopes below Devil's Peak (ABOVE), a seat of higher education for students from all over southern Africa (OPPOSITE).

JAMESON STEPS

Une vue aérienne d'une des institutions les plus respectées du pays, l'Université de Cape Town, sur le versant de Devil's Peak (CI-CONTRE). L'université est le siège d'éducation supérieure pour les nombreux étudiants qui viennent de toute l'Afrique Australe (À DROITE).

Luftaufnahme einer der respektiertesten Bildungsstätten Südafrikas, der Universität von Kapstadt, die an den Hängen der Teufelsspitze liegt (GEGENÜBER), und wo Studenten aus ganz Südafrika zur Ausbildung hinkommen (RECHTS).

MOWBRAY VENDOR

Horsepower is harnessed to bring organic vegetables to the doorsteps of residents in the quiet backstreets of Mowbray (ABOVE), while taxis (OPPOSITE) ferry passengers down Main Road towards the city. There are tens of thousands of these taxis throughout Cape Town, most of which operate principally between the sprawling townships and the city centre.

TAXI TRADE

Une charrette à cheval livre des produits agricoles biologiques aux résidents des ruelles tranquilles de Mowbray (CI-CONTRE). Plus loin, dans Main Road, les taxis transportent leurs passagers en ville (CI-DESSUS). Des dizaines de milliers de taxis sillonnent Cape Town et environs, principalement entre les townships et le centre-ville.

Um den Einwohnern von Mowbray das Biogemüse bis an die Haustür zu liefern, verwendet man noch Pferdestärke (GEGENÜBER). Die Taxen (OBEN) sammeln ihre Fahrgäste entlang der Hauptstraße, auf dem Weg in die Stadt. Es gibt Tausende solcher Taxen in Kapstadt, vorallem zwischen den ausgedehnten ‚Townships' und dem Stadtzentrum.

OBSERVATORY EATERIES

Some of Cape Town's most interesting – and most affordable – restaurants
and shops can be found among the old buildings of Observatory (known as
'Obs' by locals). Among these are Wannabee's internet café and Diva's
Restaurant (ABOVE), and the illuminated Just Because Shop (OPPOSITE).

NIGHT-TIME SHOPPING IN OBS

Quelques uns des restaurants et magasins les plus intéressants – et aux prix raisonnables – peuvent se trouver entre les vieux immeubles du quartier d'Observatory. Parmi ceux-ci sont Wannabee's Café et Diva's Restaurant (CI-CONTRE), et Just Because Shop, tout illuminé (CI-DESSUS).

Zu den interessantesten – und preiswertesten – Gaststätten und Geschäften Kapstadts zählen jene, die man in diesen alten Gebäuden in Observatory findet, wie Wannabee's Café und Diva's Restaurant (GEGENÜBER) und der hell erleuchtete Just Because Shop (OBEN).

RATANGA JUNCTION

Adrenaline junkies are guaranteed a quick fix on a variety of head-spinning rides (ABOVE and OPPOSITE) at Africa's biggest theme park, Ratanga Junction, near Cape Town. If the rides are too much for you, ease off for some relaxing shopping at nearby Canal Walk which, together with Ratanga Junction, is part of the Century City complex.

ADRENALINE RUSH

Les amateurs d'émotions fortes trouverons de quoi les satisfaire (CI-CONTRE et CI-DESSUS) à Ratanga Junction, le parc à thème le plus grand d'Afrique, près de Cape Town. Pour vous remettre de vos émotions, relaxez vous en faisant du shopping au Canal Walk tout proche, qui avec Ratanga Junction fait partie du complexe de Century City.

Wer den Nervenkitzel liebt, kommt auf seine Kosten bei den schwindeler-regenden Fahrten (OBEN und GEGENÜBER) auf dem größten Rummelplatz Afrikas, Ratanga Junction, bei Kapstadt. Wem dieserart Fahrten nicht liegen, der kann sich bei einem Einkaufsbummel im nahegelegenen Canal Walk entspannen. Ratanga Junction und Canal Walk bilden Teil des Century City Komplexes.

CANAL WALK

Canoeists messing about in boats in the waterways encircling Canal Walk (ABOVE). The largest regional shopping centre in Africa, Canal Walk forms part of the Century City complex near Cape Town. Inside the centre's domed and tiled interiors (OPPOSITE) countless eateries and more than 350 shops beckon visitors with a tantalising array of wares.

MARBLED ELEGANCE

Les canoéistes pagayent sur les canaux qui ceinturent Canal Walk, le plus grand centre commercial régional d'Afrique du Sud, qui fait partie du complexe de Century City, près de Cape Town (CI-CONTRE). Sous les coupoles du complexe, plus de 350 magasins attirent les visiteurs avec une sélection alléchante de marchandises (CI-DESSUS).

Kanufahrer paddeln auf den Kanälen, die Canal Walk umgeben. Es ist das größte regionale Einkaufszentrum in Afrika und bildet Teil des Century City Komplexes bei Kapstadt (GEGENÜBER). Unter dem Kuppeldach breitet sich ein riesiges Einkaufszentrum aus, das mit schönen Fliesen ausgelegt ist (OBEN), und wo mehr als 350 Geschäfte dem Besucher eine verführerische Warenpalette offerieren.

GRAND WEST CASINO

The promise of instant wealth lures some 10,000 visitors a day to Cape Town's R1,3-bn Grand West Casino (ABOVE). The entrance to the casino's Grand Hotel welcomes visitors with this captivating sculpture of three minstrels (OPPOSITE TOP), while slot-machines form a gaudy guard of honour inside (OPPOSITE BOTTOM).

GLAMOUR AND GLITZ

L'espoir d'une fortune subite attire quotidiennement quelques 10,000 visiteurs au Grand West Casino de Cape Town (CI-CONTRE). A l'entrée du Grand Hotel du casino, une sculpture fascinante de trois minstrels (À DROITE CI-DESSUS) accueille les visiteurs, alors qu'à l'intérieur les machines à sous forment une garde d'honneur clinquante (À DROITE CI-DESSOUS).

Die Hoffnung auf den Treffer lockt täglich 10,000 Besucher ins Grand West Kasino (GEGENÜBER). Der Eingang des Grand Hotels im Kasinokomplex heißt die Gäste mit diesem stimmungsvollen Bildhauerwerk der 'Drei Kapstädter Musikanten' willkommen (RECHTS OBEN). Innen bilden die funkelnden Spielautomaten eine grelle Ehrengarde (RECHTS UNTEN).

langa

TSOGO ENVIRONMENTAL CENTRE

While most of the working population of the township of Langa heads into Cape Town every day to work in businesses and homes, these mothers (OPPOSITE) support their families by recycling goods at Langa's Tsogo Environmental Centre. Their children (ABOVE) are cared for at crèches such as this one.

LANGA CRAFTSPEOPLE

Alors que la population active de Langa se rend chaque jour à Cape Town pour travailler, ces mères (CI-DESSUS), supportent leur famille en recyclant des articles de rejet au Tsogo Environmental Centre à Langa; pendant ce temps, une crèche s'occupera de leurs enfants (CI-CONTRE).

Die meisten Einwohner Langas verkehren tagtäglich nach Kapstadt zur Arbeit in Firmen und Haushälten, aber diese Mütter (OBEN) sorgen für den Lebensunterhalt ihrer Familien durch die Wiederverwertung von Abfallprodukten im Tsogo Umweltzentrum. Ihre Kinder werden dieweil in Kinderhorten wie diesem (GEGENÜBER) versorgt.

langa

138

HOSTEL LIFE

Luxuries are in short supply in the black township of Langa, near Cape Town, where dismal hostels such as these (ABOVE) house poor migrant workers with their sparse possessions (OPPOSITE RIGHT). Services, such as the barber (OPPOSITE LEFT), are advertised on walls and makeshift billboards.

TOWNSHIP TABLEAUX

Le township noir de Langa près de Cape Town n'offre aucun luxe; des lugubres résidences (CI-CONTRE) abritent des travailleurs saisonniers et leurs maigres possessions (CI-DESSUS À DROITE). Les services, comme le coiffeur, sont annoncés sur les murs ou par des panneaux d'affichage improvisés (CI-DESSUS À GAUCHE).

Luxusgüter sind in der schwarzen Wohnsiedlung von Langa bei Kapstadt kaum vorhanden. Hier stehen trostlose Arbeiterwohnheime (GEGENÜBER), wo arme Wanderarbeiter mit ihrem spärlichen Besitz (OBEN RECHTS) leben. Dienstleistungen, wie etwa dieser Friseur (OBEN LINKS) betreiben ihre Werbung auf Wänden und anderen Oberflächen.

HELDERBERG NATURE RESERVE

Stately mountains loom above a gay floral garden in the Helderberg Nature
Reserve (ABOVE). The Western Cape is a wonderland of nature reserves and
delightful wine estates, such as Vergelegen not far from Cape Town (OPPOSITE).

VERGELEGEN

Des montagnes imposantes dominent de plaisants champs de fleurs à Helderberg Nature Reserve (CI-CONTRE). Le Cap possède une profusion de réserves naturelles et de nombreux domaines vinicoles, comme celui de Vergelegen, proche de Cape Town (CI-DESSUS).

Stattliche Berge bilden den Hintergrund zu dem bunten Blumengarten im Helderberg Naturschutzgebiet (GEGENÜBER). Das Westkap ist eine Märchenlandschaft an Naturschutzgebieten und zauberhaften Weingütern, wie Vergelegen (OBEN), das unweit von Kapstadt liegt.

142

STRAND SEAFRONT

Golden beaches, safe bathing and excellent fishing await holiday-makers at the cosy coastal resort of the Strand (ABOVE), while the sheltered harbour at Gordon's Bay further east provides safe moorings for yachts from around the world (OPPOSITE).

GORDON'S BAY HARBOUR

La plaisante villégiature de Strand (CI-CONTRE) attire de nombreux vacan-ciers par ses plages dorées, ses baignades sans danger et sa très bonne pêche. Un peu plus à l'est, le port bien abrité de Gordon's Bay offre un excellent mouillage aux yachts qui viennent du monde entier (CI-DESSUS).

Schöne Sandstrände, sicheres Baden und gute Verhältnisse zum Angeln erwarten die Urlauber im gemütlichen Ferienort Strand (GEGENÜBER). Der geschützte Hafen von Gordon's Bay (OBEN), etwas weiter östlich gelegen, bietet einen sicheren Hafen für Jachten aus aller Welt.

THE OLD HARBOUR, HERMANUS

The nutrient-rich waters of Walker Bay surge against the old harbour wall at Hermanus (ABOVE), one of South Africa's premier whale-watching resorts. When the Southern Right whales arrive, the town's whale crier makes sure that everyone knows about it (OPPOSITE).

HERALDING THE WHALES

Les vagues de Walker Bay déferlent contre la jetée du vieux port à Hermanus (CI-CONTRE), un important site d'observation de baleines. Quand vient la saison des baleines, le crieur de la ville annonce leur arrivée à tout venant (CI-DESSUS).

Die nährstoffreichen Gewässer der Walker Bay umspülen den alten Hafenwall in Hermanus (GEGENÜBER), einem der besten Plätze in Südafrika zur Beobachtung von Walen. Wenn die Südlichen Glattwale eintreffen, sorgt der ‚Walverkünder' der Stadt dafür, daß es allen bekannt gemacht wird (OBEN).

ARNISTON

SEASIDE FUN

Fishermen leave their boats out to dry on the slipway at Arniston (OPPOSITE). Children devise their own brand of fun and games nearby (ABOVE).

Les pêcheurs tirent leurs bateaux au sec à Arniston (CI-CONTRE), pendant que près de là, leurs enfants s'amusent à leur façon (ci-dessus).

Die Fischer lassen ihre Boote auf der Gleitbahn in Arniston (GEGENÜBER) trockenen, während die Kinder lustig spielen (OBEN).

stellenbosch

148

STRAWBERRY PICKING

It's open season for strawberry pickers at Polkadraai Farm Stall near Stellenbosch every spring, where members of the public, for a small fee, can pick strawberries to their hearts' content. A mother and her son show the fruits of their labours (LEFT), while scarecrows create a colourful country pantomime around a home-made aeroplane (OPPOSITE) at the Mooiberge Strawberry Farmstall near Stellenboch.

MOOIBERGE STRAWBERRIES

C'est la saison des fraises à Polkadraai Farm Stall près de Stellenbosch, et le public peut en récolter tant qu'il veut, en échange d'un modeste droit d'entrée. Une mère et son fils montrent leur récolte (CI-CONTRE), tandis qu'à Mooiberge Strawberry Farm Stall, les épouvantails composent une pittoresque scène campagnarde, y compris un avion fait-maison (CI-DESSUS).

Erntezeit für Selbstpflücker am Polkadraai Straßenstand bei Stellenbosch. Alljährlich kann man hier im Frühjahr für ein kleines Entgeld nach Herzenslust Erdbeeren pflücken. Mutter und Sohn präsentieren den Ertrag ihrer Erntearbeit (GEGENÜBER). Vogelscheuchen bilden eine farbenfreudige Pantomime des Landlebens neben dem selbstgebastelten Flugzeug (OBEN) am Mooiberge Erdbeerstand unweit von Stellenbosch.

stellenbosch

150

LANZERAC LEGACY

The 300-year-old gabled exterior of Lanzerac Manor and Winery in the Jonkershoek Valley (ABOVE) is a proud example of early Cape Dutch craftmanship. In the cellars of one of Stellenbosch's wine farms are brandy vats and wine in storage (OPPOSITE).

BRANDY AND WINE CELLARS

Le style de la façade du manoir de Lanzerac, vieux de 300 ans, dans la Jonkershoek Valley (CI-CONTRE) est un pur exemple de la maîtrise architecturale des anciens viticulteurs du Cap. Dans les celliers d'un des anciens manoirs à Stellenbosch, on pourra voir ces réserves de vin et d'eau de vie (CI-DESSUS).

Die 300-jährige Giebelfront des Herrenhauses von Lanzerac, dem Weingut im Jonkershoektal (GEGENÜBER), liefert ein beeindruckendes Zeugnis der Baukunst dieser Zeit, als in den ersten Keltereien und Schnappsbrennereien Pionierarbeit geleistet wurde. Große Weinbrandfässer und gelagerter Flaschenwein auf einem der alten Anwesen im kapholländischen Stil bei Stellenbosch (OBEN).

franschhoek

FRANSCHHOEK VALLEY

French Huguenots, escaping religious persecution in Europe, fled to one of the most beautiful valleys in the world, the Franschhoek Valley (ABOVE), in 1688. In this region they established wine farms which flourish to this day. The Huguenot Monument in Franschhoek honours the memory of these pioneering settlers (OPPOSITE).

HUGUENOT MONUMENT

En 1688, les Huguenots français, fuyant les persécutions religieuses en Europe, trouvèrent refuge dans une des plus belles vallées du monde, la Franschhoek Valley (CI-CONTRE), où ils établirent les domaines vinicoles qui y prospèrent encore à ce jour. Le monument aux Huguenots (CI-DESSUS) fut érigé à la mémoire de ces courageux pionniers.

Französische Hugenotten, die der religiösen Verfolgung in Europa entflohen, gelangten 1688 in eines der schönsten Täler der Welt, dem Franschhoektal (GEGENÜBER), wo sie Weingüter aufbauten, die noch heute florieren. Das Hugenottendenkmal in Franschhoek gedenkt dieser Pioniere (OBEN).

PAARL ROCK

The granite domes of Paarl Rock in the Paarl Mountain Reserve tower over
the Nantes Dam (ABOVE) not far from Cape Town. Paarl, on the banks of the
Berg River, is one of the three oldest settlements in South Africa and boasts
the architectural styles of many different eras (OPPOSITE).

Les dômes de granite de Paarl Rock, dominent le réservoir de Nantes Dam (CI-CONTRE), non loin de Cape Town. Paarl, sur les rives de la Berg River, est un des trois plus anciens centres d'Afrique du Sud, et ses rues sont bordées d'immeubles appartenant à des styles architecturaux de diverses époques (À DROITE).

Die Granitkuppen des Paarl Rock im Naturschutzgebiet ragen hinter dem Nantes-Stausee auf (GEGENÜBER), der unweit von Kapstadt liegt. Paarl liegt an den Ufern des Bergflußes und zählt zu den drei ältesten Niederlassungen Südafrikas. Im Ort sieht man viele unterschiedliche Baustile aus verschiedenen Epochen (RECHTS).

LANGEBAAN LAGOON

Wild flowers greet visitors with a blaze of colour on the edge of Langebaan Lagoon (ABOVE), heart of the West Coast National Park. Dozens of inlets and tiny beaches, like this one (OPPOSITE) at the lagoon's edge, afford holiday-makers a chance to relax in the sun.

LAZY DAYS

De grandes étendues couvertes de fleurs sauvages attendent les visiteurs aux abords de la lagune de Langebaan (CI-CONTRE), au cœur du West Coast National Park. Les criques et petites plages comme celle ci (CI-DESSUS), abondent le long du littoral et permettent aux vacanciers de se délasser au soleil.

Ein Blumenteppich von Wildblumen begrüßt die Besucher am Ufer der Lagune bei Langebaan (GEGENÜBER) im Herzen des Westküsten-Nationalparks. Dutzende von kleinen Buchten und Stränden wie dieser (OBEN) säumen die Lagunenufer und bieten Urlaubern geruhsame Plätzchen in der Sonne.

PATERNOSTER

The quaint West Coast fishing village of Paternoster (ABOVE) boasts excellent catches of crayfish and perlemoen. Further north, Lambert's Bay is another flourishing fishing port. The town is well known for the huge colonies of Cape gannets that roost and breed on Bird Island (OPPOSITE) which lies approximately 100 metres offshore.

LAMBERT'S BAY CAPE GANNET COLONY

Le pittoresque village de Paternoster, sur la West Coast (CI-CONTRE), offre de riches pêches de langoustes et d'oreilles-de-mer. Plus au nord, un autre port de pêche prospère, Lambert's Bay, est notoire pour les importantes colonies de fous de Bassant qui nichent et se reproduisent à Bird Island (CI-DESSUS), à une centaine de mètres au large.

Das malerische Fischerdorf Paternoster liegt an der Westküste (GEGENÜBER). Dies ist ein ergiebiges Fanggebiet für Langusten und Abalone. Weiter nördlich trifft man auf Lambert's Bay, auch ein geschäftiger Fischerhafen und zudem bekannt für seine großen Kolonien von Kaptölpeln, die auf der etwa 100 Meter vorgelagerten Vogelinsel (OBEN) nisten und brüten.

cedarberg

160

WOLFBERG ARCH

The majesty of the Cape's Cedarberg Mountains is captured in this picture of the Wolfberg Arch.

La majesté des Cedarberg Mountains est bien rendue dans cette photo du Wolfberg Arch.

Der imposante Felsbogen, Wolfberg Arch, vermittelt einen Eindruck der majestätischen Zederberge.